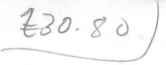

£30.80

GRADE

4

The Syllabus of Examinations shoulc
requirements, especially those for :
sight-reading. Attention should bε
Notices on the inside front cover, v
of any changes.

The syllabus is obtainable from n.
The Associated Board of the Royal Schools of Music,
14 Bedford Square, London WC1B 3JG (please send a
stamped addressed C5 (162mm × 229mm) envelope).

In examination centres outside the UK, information and
syllabuses may be obtained from the Local Representative.

GW00362156

CONTENTS

Where appropriate, pieces in this volume have been checked with original source material
and edited as necessary for instructional purposes. Fingering, phrasing, bowing,
metronome marks and the editorial realization of ornaments (where given) are for
guidance but are not comprehensive or obligatory.

**DO NOT
PHOTOCOPY
© MUSIC**

Alternative pieces for this grade

Music origination by Jack Thompson.
Cover by Økvik Design.
Printed in England by Halstan & Co. Ltd,
Amersham, Bucks.

11th July
Friday
7.00 Andants

Scottish Brawl

A:1

Arranged by
Edward Huws Jones

ANON.

Brawl is the English form of the French word 'Branle', which meant a swaying dance, immensely popular throughout Europe in the 16th century. The source for *Scottish Brawl* is a collection by Attaingnant – a music publisher who collected dance music for a series of books printed between 1530 and 1557. The piece needs to be played with relentless rhythmic energy! EHJ

Rondo

Fifth movement from Divertimento No. 2 in B flat
K. Anh. 229 No. 2 / K. 439b

Transcribed and edited by
Richard Jones

MOZART

[Allegro ♩ = c.108]

This Rondo is taken from the second of five Divertimenti, written as trios for two basset horns (or clarinets) and bassoon in Vienna probably around 1783. Enjoy the contrast in articulation – much of the piece is legato in character, but with some witty (even cheeky!) phrases. Inconsistencies in slurring have been corrected. The dynamics in bars 100 (piano) and 101 (violin), and from *cresc.* in bars 117 (piano) and 119 (violin) to *f* in bar 121 (piano and violin) are editorial suggestions only. The *rall.* and subsequent *a tempo* in bars 120 and 121 have also been added by the editor. Some additional or alternative articulation marks have been added by analogy with the composer's.

Source: *Trois Sérénades* (Bonn, Simrock, 1812).

AB 2748

Gigue
Fifth movement from Ouverture in D, BWV 1068

Transcribed and edited by
Richard Jones

J. S. BACH

This rollicking Gigue is the finale of Bach's Orchestral Suite in D: a joyful conclusion which was originally written for three trumpets, timpani, two oboes, strings and continuo. All dynamics, the articulation marks in bars 18–20 and the appoggiaturas in bars 48 and 50 are editorial suggestions only. Some slurs have been added by analogy with the composer's.

© 2000 by The Associated Board of the Royal Schools of Music

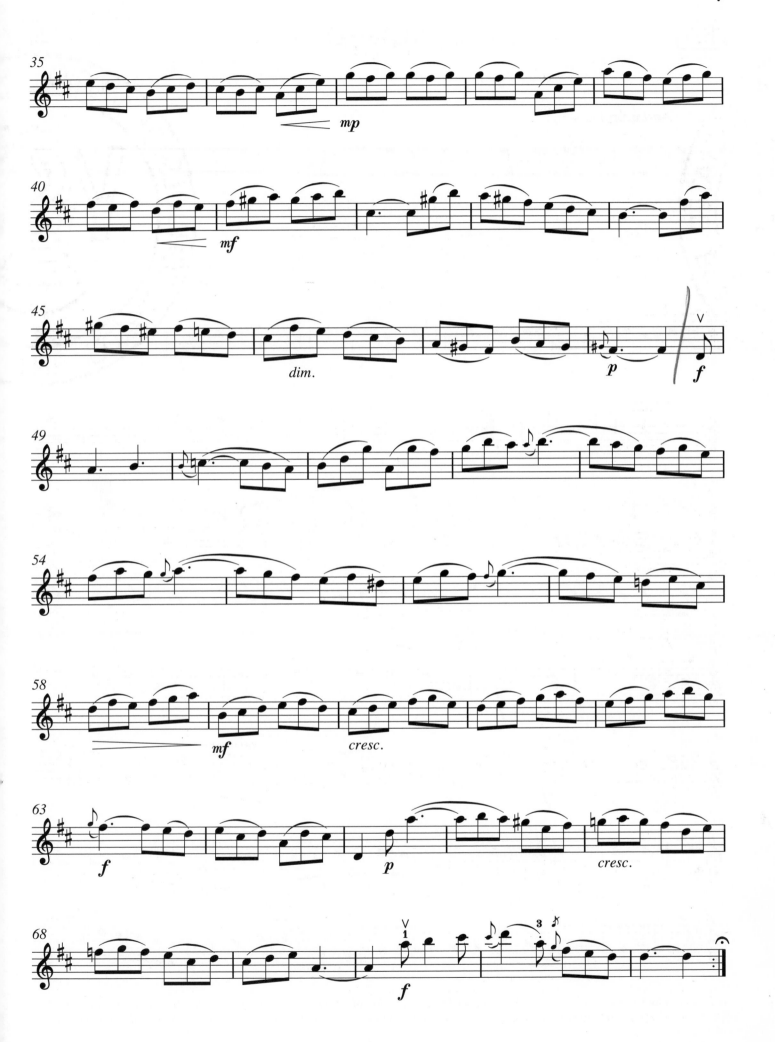

B:1

La Cinquantaine

GABRIEL-MARIE

Reproduced for sale in France, Belgium, Italy and Spain by permission of Editions Gérard Billaudot, Paris/United Music Publishers Ltd
All enquiries for this piece apart from the examinations should be addressed to United Music Publishers Ltd, 42 Rivington Street, London EC2A 3BN.

AB 2748

B:2

Ballet Music No. 2
from *Rosamunde*, Op. 26, D. 797

Arranged by
Howard Ferguson

SCHUBERT

Schubert wrote nearly 20 theatrical works, few of which were performed during his lifetime. One exception was *Rosamunde, Princess of Cyprus* (1823), a romantic drama by the authoress Wilhelmina von Chézy with incidental music by Schubert. Although the drama was badly received and survives only as a synopsis of the plot, the incidental music, from which the above piece is taken, has become one of Schubert's most popular orchestral works.

B:3

Waltz

No. 8 from *Ten Progressive Tunes*

SOMERVELL

© 1919 Stainer & Bell Ltd
Reproduced by permission. All enquiries for this piece apart from the examinations should be addressed to Stainer & Bell Ltd, PO Box 110, Victoria House, 23 Gruneisen Road, London N3 1DZ.

Stormy Weather

Arranged by Roy Stratford,
Edward Huws Jones and Alan Gout

ARLEN

This piece is a jazz classic from the 1930s. It should be played in swing rhythm throughout – that is, pairs of quavers and dotted rhythms are all played as easy triplets. This applies to the accompaniment too. Listen to recordings of some of the great jazz violinists such as Stephane Grappelli or Joe Venuti to develop a sense of the style. EHJ

Words and Music by Harold Arlen and Ted Koehler. © 1933 EMI Mills Music Inc., USA. 50% print rights controlled by Warner Bros Publications, USA/International Music Publications Ltd, 50% by Redwood Music Ltd, London NW1 8BD.
Reproduced by permission of International Music Publications Ltd. All enquiries for this piece apart from the examinations should be addressed to International Music Publications Ltd, Griffin House, 161 Hammersmith Road, London W6 8BS.

Moderato

No. 1 from *Intermezzo*

MARTINŮ

D. C. al Fine

Copyright 1965 by Edition Bärenreiter Praha
Reproduced by permission. All enquiries for this piece apart from the examinations should be addressed to Bärenreiter Ltd, Burnt Mill, Elizabeth Way, Harlow, Essex CM20 2HX.

AB 2748

Dance

No. 2 from Ballet Suite No. 1

C:3

Arranged by
Fortunatov

SHOSTAKOVICH

Between 1949 and 1953 Shostakovich's friend and colleague Lev Atovmyan created four ballet suites for orchestra, using music assembled from some of the composer's ballet, stage and film scores. *Dance* originally comes from the ballet *The Limpid Stream*, Op. 39 (1934–5).

Checklist of Scales and Arpeggios

Candidates and teachers may find this checklist useful in learning the requirements of the grade. Full details of the forms of the various requirements, including details of rhythms, starting notes and bowing patterns, are given in the syllabus and in the scale books published by the Board.

Grade 4

			separate bows					slurred					
Major Scales								*two beats to a bow*					
	Ab **Major**	2 Octaves											
	A Major	2 Octaves											
	Bb **Major**	2 Octaves											
	C Major	2 Octaves											
	D Major	2 Octaves											
Minor Scales (*melodic* or *harmonic*)								*two beats to a bow*					
	A Minor	2 Octaves											
	B Minor	2 Octaves											
	C Minor	2 Octaves											
	D Minor	2 Octaves											
Chromatic Scales								*four notes to a bow*					
	on A	1 Octave											
	on E	1 Octave											
	on B	1 Octave											
Major Arpeggios								*three notes to a bow*					
	Ab **Major**	2 Octaves											
	A Major	2 Octaves											
	Bb **Major**	2 Octaves											
	C Major	2 Octaves											
	D Major	2 Octaves											
Minor Arpeggios								*three notes to a bow*					
	A Minor	2 Octaves											
	B Minor	2 Octaves											
	C Minor	2 Octaves											
	D Minor	2 Octaves											
Dominant Sevenths								*four notes to a bow*					
	in D	1 Octave											
	in A	1 Octave											
	in E	1 Octave											

Printed by
Halstan & Co. Ltd., Amersham, Bucks.

3/00